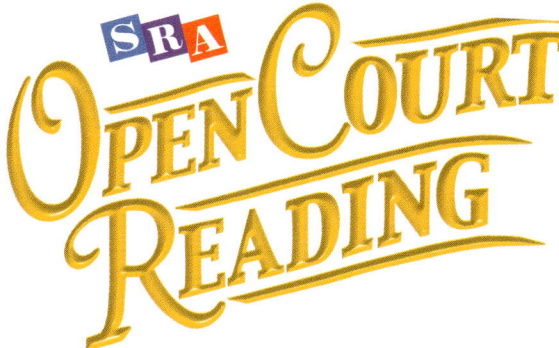

The Cold Troll

A Division of The McGraw·Hill Companies

Columbus, Ohio

www.sra4kids.com

SRA/McGraw-Hill
A Division of The **McGraw·Hill** Companies

Copyright © 2002 by SRA/McGraw-Hill.

All rights reserved. Except as permitted under the United States Copyright Act, no part of this publication may be reproduced or distributed in any form or by any means, or stored in a database or retrieval system, without prior written permission from the publisher.

Printed in the United States of America.

Send all inquiries to:
SRA/McGraw-Hill
8787 Orion Place
Columbus, OH 43240-4027

ISBN 0-07-569728-9
3 4 5 6 7 8 9 DBH 05 04 03 02

Jake Troll's old home felt cold.
It was so cold that ice formed on his nose.
It was so cold that his stove froze.

Jake Troll poked his broken stove with a stick.
"This is no joke," Jake Troll said.
"This cold is too much. I have one last hope.
I will go drop a note for Mole."

Mole had a nice snug hole.
Cold Jake Troll left a note.
He slipped the note into Mole's hole.

Mole read Jake Troll's note.
"Do not mope, Troll," Mole scolded.
"Take home this robe."

Jake Troll went home and put on his robe.
For once, Jake Troll had no ice on his nose.
"I am not cold!" yelled Jake Troll.
"Thank you, Mole!"